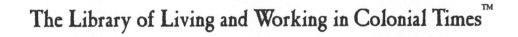

A Day in the Life of a Colonial Printer

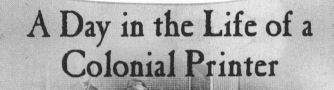

Kathy Wilmore

...Publishing Group's

...owerKids Press™

New York

To Bryan Brown, for the encouragement, humor, and grace that helped so much as I wrote this book—
and to my mother, Julia C. Wilmore, who got me started.

Published in 2000 by The Rosen Publishing Group, Inc.
29 East 21st Street, New York, NY 10010

Copyright © 2000 by The Rosen Publishing Group, Inc.

First Edition
Book design: Danielle Primiceri

Photo Credits: Cover © The Granger Collection, New York and North Wind Pictures; pp. 4, 8, 11, 16, 19 © The Granger Collection, New York; pp. 7, 15 © 1997 North Wind Pictures; p. 12 © 1998 North Wind Pictures; p. 20 © 1995 North Wind Pictures.

Wilmore, Kathy.
    A day in the life of a Colonial printer / Kathy Wilmore.
        p. cm. — (The library of living and working in Colonial times)
    Includes index.
    Summary: Describes a day in the life of a Colonial printer, the workings of a printing press, and how it was used to spread news.
    ISBN 0-8239-5428-5 (lib. bdg.)
    1. Printing—United States—History—18th Century—Juvenile literature. [1. Printing—History—18th century.]
    I. Title. II. Series.
Z208 .W75 1999
686.2'0973—dc21   98-49767
                                                                                   CIP
                                                                                    AC

Manufactured in the United States of America
Joseph Clarke and his shop are fictional, but the details in this story about Colonial printers and Colonial life are true.

Contents

Colonial America

For a printer like Joseph Clarke, life in Colonial America was full of excitement. A printer was in charge of making the newspapers, and there was plenty of news being made at this time. In the early 1600s, many English people came to America to live in **colonies**. These colonies were ruled by England, but soon the people in the colonies decided that they wanted to become an **independent** country. Newspapers helped spread ideas about America's freedom.

◀ *These colonists from New York read newspapers in a coffeehouse reading room.*

Meet Mr. Clarke

Joseph Clarke became a printer the way most people did. When he was a boy, his parents sent him to work in a printer's shop. He served there as an **apprentice** for ten years. When he was 21 years old, Joseph Clarke moved to the colony called Maryland, to work for a wealthy printer. Mr. Clarke did so well there that he earned enough money to open his own shop. He became the proud owner of Clarke's Post and Printing.

Benjamin Franklin, Colonial America's most famous printer, at his printing press. ▶

"Stop the Press!"

When a Colonial business owner wanted more **customers**, he did what people do today. He went to a printer and put an **ad** in the newspaper. If the businessman could not read or write, he told the printer what he wanted the ad to say.

Sometimes, a messenger brought news to the printer's shop. A messenger told Mr. Clarke that a ship had just arrived, bringing important news. A new law said that American colonists had to pay higher **taxes** to England's king.

◄ *A printer and his apprentice get ready to print the latest news.*

9

The Press Room

Like many Colonial printers, Mr. Clarke ran a bookstore and post office, as well as a printing business. His press room was in the back. There were tables for cutting and stacking paper. Special cases held blocks of **type**. Each block had one letter carved into it. Jugs of ink stood near a wood-burning stove. The ink was kept warm by the stove to keep it from getting too thick and sticky. The biggest thing in the room was the **printing press**.

This Colonial printer gets the press ready for printing. ▶

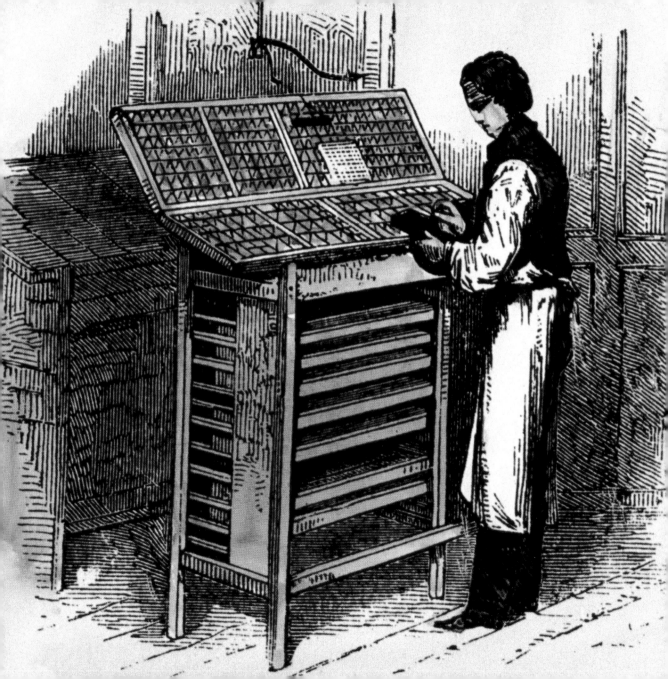

Putting It Together

Mr. Clarke told his apprentice and his **assistant** that he wanted to put a new story on the front page of the paper. Mr. Clarke and his apprentice sorted quickly through the cases of type blocks to find the letters they needed. They spelled out the words of the story, one letter at a time, by lining up the type blocks in a special tray. When they had put together enough type to fill half a page, the apprentice tied the blocks of letters into place. Then he took the tray to the assistant.

◀ *This apprentice chooses blocks of type to spell out a story.*

Blocking and Inking

Caleb, the assistant, took a jug of ink from next to the stove. He mixed the ink to make it smooth. Then, using two pads covered with leather, he smeared ink onto the tray of type. The apprentice put a sheet of paper into a frame on the press. Then he turned the giant screw on the press. It squeezed the paper and the inky tray of type together.

A printer's apprentice turns the screw that presses inky type against paper. ▶

Putting Words to Paper

After unscrewing the press, the printer, apprentice, and assistant inspected their work. If the top half of a page looked okay, they put the page on a rack to dry. They printed more sheets the same way, first inking, then pressing. The printer filled another type tray for the bottom half of the page. Like most printers, Mr. Clarke used more than just letters in his printing. Some of his type blocks had designs cut into them. He used a flowery pattern in the business owner's ad to make it stand out.

◀ *The apprentice prepares the paper while the assistant inks the type.*

A Long Process

The apprentice and assistant printed the bottom halves of the dried sheets. Then Mr. Clarke's wife brought lunch, so the men took a short break.

After lunch, Mr. Clarke filled two more trays of type, one for each half of the back page. The apprentice and assistant inked and pressed, until both sides of all the sheets were done. Luckily, Mr. Clarke's newspaper was only two pages long. If they worked hard and fast, they could print 200 copies in an hour.

A printer and his assistant fill trays with blocks of type. ▶

"Here Comes the Post Rider!"

Post riders carried letters and news from colony to colony on horseback. Mr. Clarke had a stack of newspapers ready for the post rider to take away. Colonists everywhere would be interested in his story about the new taxes.

To stay in business, Mr. Clarke wrote his newspaper for everyone. He served people loyal to the king of England, as well as those who wanted independence. His article described the taxes. It did not say whether they were good or bad.

◀ *A post rider announces that he's arriving with mail.*

The Next Edition

Colonial printers did more than print newspapers. They also printed signs for shopkeepers, invitations to special events, and official notices for the government. By the end of his workday, a Colonial printer had heard enough news from his customers to start writing another **edition** of his newspaper.

Web Sites:

Due to the changing nature of Internet links, PowerKids Press has developed an online list of Web sites related to the subject of this book. This site is updated regularly. Please use this link to access the list: www.powerkidslinks.com/llwct/dlcpri/

Glossary

ad (AD) Something that describes what you are selling.

apprentice (uh-PREN-tis) A young person learning a skill or trade.

assistant (uh-SIS-tint) Someone who helps.

colonies (KAH-luh-neez) Areas in a new land to which large groups of people move, but which remain under the rule of their old country.

customers (KUS-tuh-murz) People who buy goods or services.

edition (uh-DIH-shun) A number of copies of a newspaper or book that is printed at one time.

independent (in-dih-PEN-dint) Free from the control, support, influence, or help of others.

printing press (PRIN-ting PRES) A machine used to print many copies of something.

taxes (TAK-siz) Money that people give to the government to help pay for public services.

type (TYP) A block with a letter carved into it, used in a printing press to print newspapers or books.

Index